The Eagle's Mandate

Benjamin Williams, Jr.

Copyright © 2020 by Benjamin Williams

All rights reserved. No part of this book may be reproduced or used in any manner without written permission of the copyright owner except for the use of quotations in a book review. For more information, address:
Realtalkben@gmail.com

FIRST EDITION

Realtalkben@gmail.com

This book is dedicated to the dreamers all across the nation. The hard workers and hustlers that are determined to change themselves and families lives for the better. You are the most incredible creation God has ever made. The world awaits your skills, talents, and impact. So never give up, move by faith, and leave your mark on world by becoming the best version of yourself!

Table of Contents

Introduction 1

The Eagle's Determination: The Ability to Fly; Leave the Nest of Safety 2

The Eagle's Focus: Confidence Over Uncertainty 3

The Eagle's Overview: Mind Over Circumstances; Determination vs. Disappointment 4

The Eagle's Experience: Learned Behavior: Stay in Your Lane; Stick to What You Know 5

The Eagle's Creativity: Changing Direction When Necessary; Do Not Fly Into a Wall 6

The Eagle's Vision: Roadmap to Success; Plan, Review, and Execute Your Goals 7

The Eagle's Convocation (A group of Eagles); Demand Like Minds and Similar Outcomes 8

The Eagle's Thought Process: Spot Your Target; Swoop and Conquer 9

The Eagle's Monogamous Nature: The Ability to Exercise Self-control; a Risky Proposition 10

The Eagle's Motivational Drive: What Drives You? The Winning Attitude; Train Your Mind 11

Final Thought 12

Your Personal Journal 13

    How Will You Make Sure That Your Leadership Style is Captivating and Enlightening? 15
    Eagle's Leadership Qualities 16
    Overcoming Your Past; Embracing the Future 17
    Next Steps 18

Introduction

At a young age, I was often curious and questioned how things worked. I also discovered that I was extremely creative and had a vast imagination. At ten years old, I was intrigued by how people were able to create an abundant lifestyle and wealth. I can remember saying things like that car is only a hundred and fifty thousand dollars in the early '90s with a straight face. The people I talked to, would reply as if something were wrong with me. It seemed to me like it was a small number.

When I turned 18, I knew something great would happen in my life, and was determined to change my circumstances for the better. I began to study self personal development books and audiotapes. One of the most profound ones that stuck out to me was "Think and Grow Rich" by Napoleon Hill. For those that have not heard of this book, it has been around for many years, and I believe it has every principle for a person to create the life that they desire. It has inspired me to write the book you are now about to read. Thank you for choosing my book to begin your new path to your life's desires, hopefully.

The Eagle's Determination: The Ability to Fly; Leave the Nest of Safety

Desire- "A strong feeling of wanting to have something or wishing for something."

Every successful person started with a desire to achieve something. Most of the time, successful people have a passion, which is definite; they decide on what they must have and burn all bridges of retreat. Therefore, the only option is to win!

What is your burning desire? What must you have in life?

_____
_____
_____
_____
_____
_____
_____
_____
_____
_____
_____

The Eagle's Focus: Confidence Over Uncertainty

Faith- "Complete trust or confidence in someone or something."

All successful people trust and believe that they will achieve their goals even when there is no evidence. The only known method to develop/grow the emotion of faith is through repetition of affirmations. What are you saying to yourself daily? How you direct your sail will be the direction of your life. It would be best if you spoke a positive experience into your desire, whether you believe it or not. If you talk positively about what you desire as present tense, ways and opportunities will come about to make it a reality. Example: I am a millionaire. Opportunities will come forth that will lead to a million-dollar income. Please do not put a time limit on it. God/Universe knows the best time and way to make your wishes reality.

Write down some affirmations for your desires.

_____

_____

_____

_____

_____

*TIP: Read them as often as possible, especially waking in the morning and just before bed.

The Eagle's Overview: Mind Over Circumstances; Determination vs. Disappointment

Auto suggestion - "The hypnotic or subconscious adoption of an idea that one has originated oneself, e.g., through repetition or verbal statements to oneself to change behavior."

The dominating thoughts one holds in his/her mind will eventually reach the subconscious mind and reproduce themselves physically in that person's life. You have two parts of your mind: the conscious and the subconscious. The conscious, which is our awareness aspect of our mental processing that we can think and talk about rationally. Our subconscious mind, which is an unquestioning creative mind that only says yes to the information it is given. This is where auto suggestion comes into play. Your subconscious is listening to everything you say, think, and feel whether it is true or not. You MUST give your subconscious instructions repeatedly. If it's a house you want, you must look at pictures of that house, and go see that house in the physical if possible. Picture yourself living in that house. Remember, the subconscious does not know the difference between real and fake; it is only saying yes and creates situations and circumstances that match your dominating thoughts and feelings.

Make a detailed list of what you desire.

_____
_____
_____
_____
_____

The Eagle's Experience: Learned Behavior: Stay in Your Lane; Stick to What You Know

Specialized Knowledge

Specialized knowledge- "someone or something trained or delivered for a particular purpose or area of knowledge."

What special skills or talents do you have or would like to have?

_____
_____
_____
_____
_____

Can that knowledge or talent create an opportunity with a definite end result when you put it into action?

_____
_____
_____
_____
_____

*TIP: Many people mistake knowledge as power. Knowledge is potential power. It is power only when used for a definite plan of action and a particular end.

The Eagle's Creativity: Changing Direction When Necessary; Do Not Fly Into a Wall

Imagination

Imagination-"The act or power of forming a mental image of something not present to the senses or never before wholly perceived in reality; creative ability."

-Webster's Dictionary

A man or woman can create anything that he or she can imagine. Your subconscious mind is receptive to all ideas that it is given. Whether it is physical or in memory, you must create a clear mental picture of what you want and hold on to this picture as often as possible. Your subconscious mind connects to a source that knows all the answers. We call that source: God/The Universe." Once the idea is given to the subconscious mind, and it is accepted, it becomes a physical reality. Situations, circumstances, and events occur that make this imagined picture tangible. It would be best if you also moved towards the vision with action work.

What do you picture daily? Do you have a clear mental picture of what you desire in mind?

_____
_____
_____
_____

*TIP: Please write down your desires and create a movie in your imagination and play it as often as possible.

The Eagle's Vision: Roadmap to Success; Plan, Review, and Execute Your Goals

Organized planning- "The ability to create and use logical, systematic processes to achieve goals."

The principles touched on in the previous chapters can now be used to make your desire(s) a reality. Align yourself with as many people as possible that can help contribute to making your dreams materialize. Be sure that each person (explained in the next chapter) has a definite role that benefits the team. Plan to meet with everyone at least twice a week. Write out a full plan of how you intend to achieve your goals. Assign a task for each person in the group and make sure the goal is attainable for each individual. Do not be afraid to make new plans if you meet failure.

_____
_____
_____
_____
_____

***TIP:** I (author) recommend referring to this chapter in "Think and Grow Rich."

The Eagle's Convocation (A group of Eagles); Demand Like Minds and Similar Outcomes

Power of the Mastermind Group

Mastermind group - a peer to peer monitoring concept used to help members solve their problems with input and advice from the other group members.

The Mastermind Group is a compelling and essential part of succeeding. When a focused group comes together for a common goal, a "Superpower is born." For example, you have a group of batteries together as opposed to one single cell alone. The group of batteries produces an even higher power. When people come together, the energies of the all minds are intensified.
When this happens, ideas flow smoothly and quickly. Every great leader understands the importance of a Mastermind group. Find individuals that are like-minded and help them discover why it would be beneficial for them to be a part of your group.

Who in your circle qualifies to be a part of your Mastermind Group? What can they contribute?
_____
_____
_____
_____
_____

The Eagle's Thought Process: Spot Your Target; Swoop and Conquer

Decision – "A conclusion or resolution reached after consideration."

Deciding on what you want in life is vital! A person that does not make a sound decision, waivers and procrastinates because they do not have a real target. Studies show that successful people make decisions quickly. Not so successful people make decisions slowly and are quick to change their minds. Today, determine what you want. Many decisions take courage, but the man or woman willing to decide holds the key to economic freedom.

What do you want?

_____

_____

_____

What are the pros and cons?

_____

_____

_____

Can the decision be reversed?

_____

_____

_____

The Eagle's Monogamous Nature: The Ability to Exercise Self-control; a Risky Proposition

Sex Transmutation

Sex transmutation – "is directing the mind from thoughts of physical expression to thoughts of another creative effort."

Sex controls the lives of many men/women. The notion that sex can either cripple a man/woman or raise them to genius. The force/energy of sexual emotion is powerful, and often, many are not able to control their desire to indulge. Still, the man/woman who learns to gain control of his/her emotions can use the energy to benefit themselves. Many have lost power due to sexual addiction. When you desire to have sex; stop and think about your goals. The thought frequency that your brain transmits is exceptionally high when you have a sexual urge. Therefore, making it easier to manifest one's desires. (Note: Refer to "Think and Grow Rich" and YouTube "Sex Transmutation for more details.)

*TIP: Next time you are aroused, redirect that energy into something constructive to achieve your goals.

The Eagle's Motivational Drive: What Drives You? The Winning Attitude; Train Your Mind

Subconscious mind

Subconscious mind- "of or concerning the part of the mind which one is not fully aware of, but which influences one's actions and feelings.

The subconscious mind, I believe, is the God in you. It is the most powerful part of the brain that not many know about it. You are the most incredible machine on the face of the earth, and your mind power is infinite. The subconscious mind has a program that comes from your parent's experiences, surroundings and everything that you learned. By the age of seven years old, the foundation of your core beliefs is created. If you do not like the results in your life, you can change them. It may take time, but it is possible.

The subconscious mind can be re-programmed with a series of techniques:

- repeat affirmations in the morning when you first awake and just before going to sleep

- listen to audios of new programs you want to download in your brain while sleeping

- get out of your comfort zone

- experience things you desire to create the emotion

Final Thought

What is the difference between eagles and other birds of prey? Eagles fly high over the clouds and focuses on it's target.

Your Personal Journal

Use this space to chronical your experience. Write out your Business Plan and all resources needed to accomplish that goal.

How Will You Make Sure That Your Leadership Style is Captivating and Enlightening?

Which style best describes you: Provider, Collaborator, Enabler or Kingmaker?

_____

_____

_____

_____

_____

_____

_____

_____

Eagle's Leadership Qualities

No Fear, Determined Mentors and Visionaries; do you measure up?

Overcoming Your Past; Embracing the Future

Are you ready to do the hard work necessary to win?

Next Steps

Find a Mentor: Historical, Author or Business Executive to follow. Write the rationale for this choice.

Social Media Contact Information:

Instagram: iambenwilliamsjr

You Tube: Realtalk Ben

Facebook: Benjamin Williams

Email: RealtalkBen@gmail.com

www.ingramcontent.com/pod-product-compliance
Lightning Source LLC
Chambersburg PA
CBHW081352040426
42450CB00015B/3404